Published in the UK by
POWERFRESH Limited
3 Gray Street
Northampton
NN1 3QQ

Telephone 44 01604 30996
Facsimile 44 01604 21013

WE'RE GETTING MARRIED
ISBN   1 874125 44 9

Printed in the UK by Avalon Print Northampton
      Powerfresh June 1995

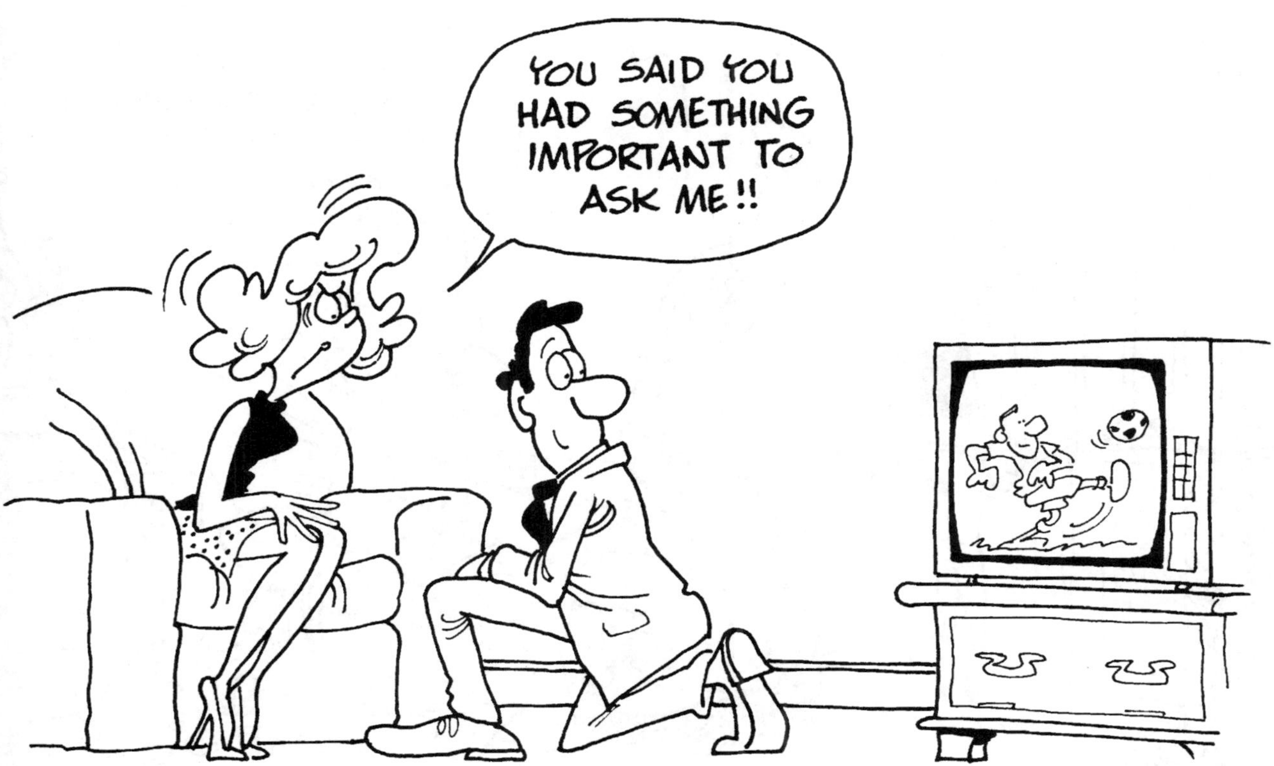
YOU SAID YOU HAD SOMETHING IMPORTANT TO ASK ME !!

MODERN MARRIAGE VOWS

DO YOU PROMISE TO LOVE HIM FOR RICHER, AND IN HEALTH, NOT FORSAKING ALL OTHERS, UNTIL YOU GET PISSED-OFF AND SEEK A DIVORCE?

LOOK ON THE BRIGHT SIDE — WE'RE NOT LOSING A DAUGHTER, WE'RE GAINING A BATHROOM!
L

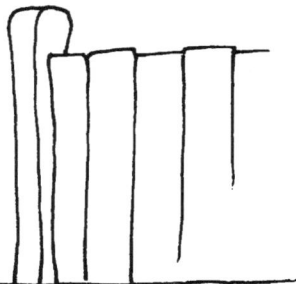

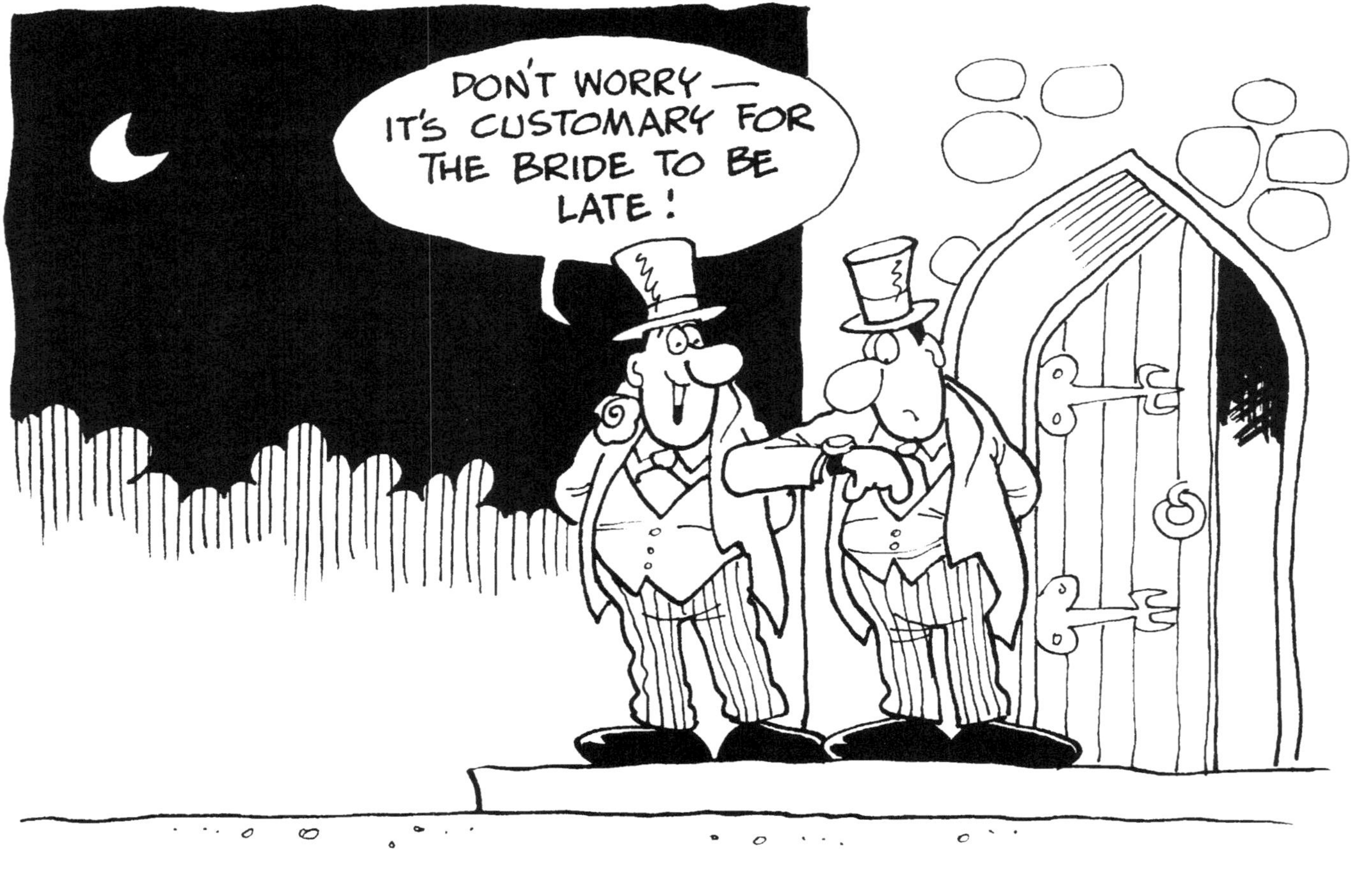
DON'T WORRY — IT'S CUSTOMARY FOR THE BRIDE TO BE LATE !

TITLES BY

POWERFRESH
· NORTHAMPTON · ENGLAND ·

Please Send Me:

Title	Price	QTY	Title	Price	QTY
CRINKLED 'N' WRINKLED	£2.99		IT'S NO FUN BEING A MOTHER	£2.99	
DRIVEN CRAZY	£2.99		WE'RE GETTING MARRIED	£2.99	
OH NO ITS XMAS AGAIN	£2.99		MONSTERS	£2.99	
TRUE LOVE	£2.99		THE ART OF SLOBOLOGY	£2.99	
IT'S A BOY	£2.99		THE DEFINITIVE GUIDE TO VASECTOMY	£2.99	
IT'S A GIRL	£2.99		KEEP FIT WITH YOUR CAT	£2.99	
NOW WE ARE 40	£2.99		MARITAL BLISS AND OTHER OXYMORONS	£2.99	
FUNNY SIDE OF 40 HIM	£2.99		THE OFFICE FROM HELL	£2.99	
FUNNY SIDE OF 40 HER	£2.99		PMT CRAZED	£2.99	
FUNNY SIDE OF 50 HIM	£2.99		SEXY CROTCHWORD PUZZLES	£2.99	
FUNNY SIDE OF 50 HER	£2.99		STONED AGE MAN	£2.99	
FUNNY SIDE OF 60'S	£2.99		OUT TO LUNCH	£2.99	
FUNNY SIDE OF SEX	£2.99		HORNY MAN'S ADULT DOODLE BOOK	£2.50	
THE COMPLETE BASTARDS GUIDE TO GOLF	£2.99		HORNY GIRL'S ADULT DOODLE BOOK	£2.50	

I have enclosed cheque / postal order for £ .... made payable to **GUNNERS**

NAME..ADDRESS..

....

COUNTY..POSTCODE..

Please return to: **Powerfresh Ltd. 3 Gray Street, Northampton, NN1 3QQ, ENGLAND.**
EEC countries please add £1 Postage, Packaging & Order processing. Outside EEC please add £3.00